REFLECTING LIGHT INTO DARK PLACES

"I was so impacted by the story of Alexander Papaderos when I first discovered it, that I read it again and again. His metaphor of the mirror and the meaning of life taught me that even in my broken and fragmented state I could seek and reflect light into the world. It is my hope that you may also be inspired as you experience this remarkable true story of Alexander Papaderos and his mission to reflect light into dark places."

Kirk A Weisler, Chief Morale Officer

ACKNOWLEDGMENTS

Reflecting upon why this book came to be written is detailed in the epilogue—But how it came to be written is through the encouraging support, assistance and expertise of the following wonderful people:

Marcos Ortega, a wonderful neighbor and friend who accompanied me all the way to Greece at his own expense to help me find and connect with Alexander Papaderos.

Shane Lealos, who discovered that Papaderos was still alive, and found the email address to get things started.

Bill Burgess the 5th, who created all of the beautiful artwork for this book and for my book The Dog Poop Initiative.

George Curtis, from Aspen Press, who has printed all of my books and been a dear friend for 20 years.

David Dolberg, who assisted with the layout and design, tapping only the smallest part of his immense creativity, talent and expertise…

Brittany, our eldest daughter, a great editor and fearless in offering her feedback to help make Dad's stuff better.

Most importantly, to my incomparable wife Rebecca Weisler, who lovingly supported my inconvenient and expensive trip to the Mediterranean shores of Crete to meet with a stranger from a story I loved, on the mere hopes that I would be able to take that story and share it with the world. Thank you my love. You are a light in my world and the love of my life.

ABOUT THE AUTHOR

Chief Morale Officer Kirk Weisler is an expert at creating outrageously cool workplace cultures and high performance teams. Over the past 20 years over 50,000 Leaders from organizations including Delta, MAYO Clinic, Johns Hopkins, YUM Brands, Bausch & Lomb, Panasonic, Coca Cola, have specifically sought Kirk's advice and wisdom on building teams, strengthening leaders and improving workplace culture. Impressively nearly 100% of Kirk's work comes from word of mouth referrals.

His unique background as a US Army Ranger, a member of the 19th Special Forces Chaplaincy, his work with At-Risk Youth and experience as a Master Storyteller & Team Builder make him a very fun, engaging, and sought-after speaker. He authored the *Best Smelling Book*, *The Dog Poop Initiative* and the semi –sweet best smeller, *The Cookie Thief*. Kirk lives in Phoenix, Arizona with "Wonderful wife Rebecca and their six remarkable children."

ABOUT THE EDITOR

Thomas Cantrell is known for his ability to hear what authors want to say and help them say it the way they really mean to say it. He is an author and speaker in his own right, his greatest calling, however, is to empower others to change the world by saying the right thing at the right time to the right people in the right way.

SHARE IT WITH OTHERS

For additional copies, or to order from our website, go to:

kirkweisler.com

For special or bulk orders, please e-mail at:

team@kirkweisler.com
or text to
678-296-9278

For speaking engagement inquiries visit us at kirkweisler.com
or contact a team member at team@kirkweisler.com

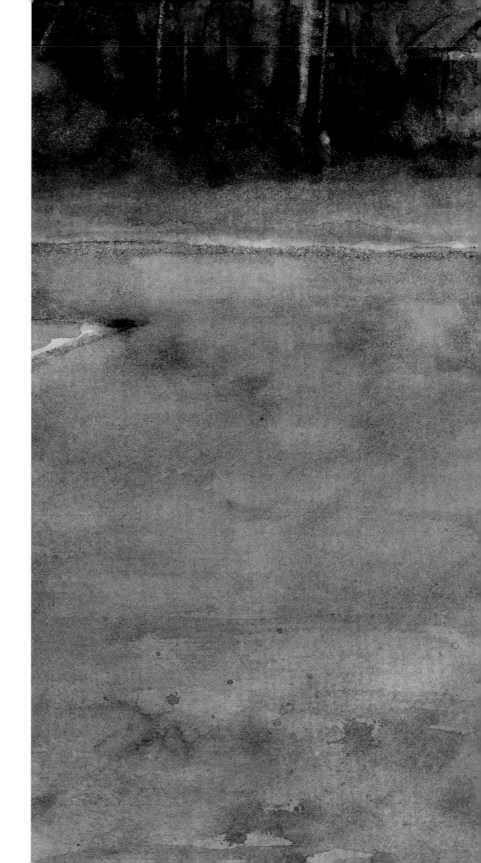

It was Career Day at school.

Many professionals visited the school to help the students begin thinking about what they might want to do when they grew up. There were doctors, firefighters, game designers, realtors, soldiers... even the Mayor was there!

They shared stories about what they did every day, why they chose their careers, and how their work brought a sense of meaning and purpose to their lives and to the world.

All the way home, Joshua and his brother Jacob talked about what they wanted to do when they grew up. They simply couldn't decide.

When the boys got home, they were excited to find that Grandpa was there.

"Grandpa, Grandpa! How did you know what you wanted to do when you grew up?" asked Joshua.

"Good question! Maybe there's an even better question to ask," Grandpa said, pulling a picture book off the shelf.

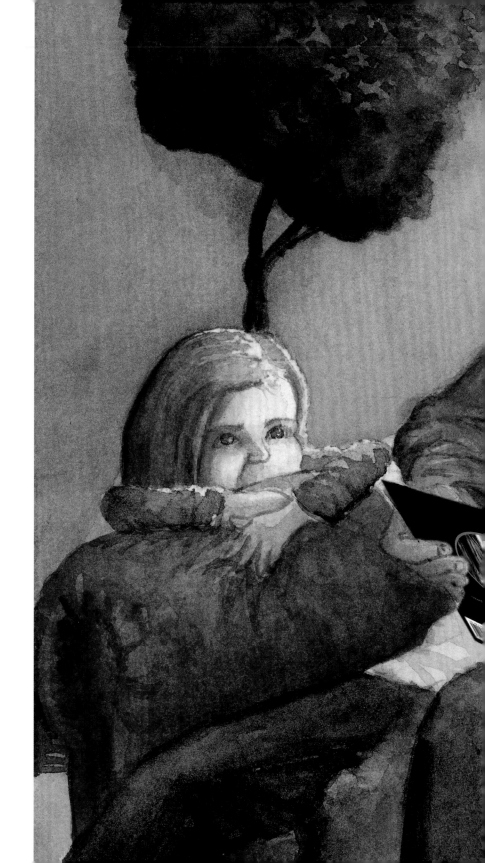

hat do you mean 'a better question'?" Jacob asked.

"Hold on boys," smiled Grandpa. "First let me share a story with you and your sister that I read to your father when he was about your age and asked me the very same question. It's a true story of a boy named Alexander Papaderos."

Grandpa opened the book and began to read ...

"ALEXANDER'S MIRROR"

My name is Alexander Papaderos. As a young boy, my family was very poor. We lived in a small village on the island of Crete in the Mediterranean Sea, not far from Greece. It was during world War II when the Nazis had tried to conquer the world – and almost did.

One day, while playing with a friend, I found a military motorcycle that had been wrecked and abandoned. There were pieces of broken mirror scattered about.

I tried to find all the pieces of the mirror and put them together, but it wasn't possible; so I kept the largest one and began to play with it.

I was fascinated at how it caught the rays of the sun, and reflected a bright patch of light wherever I aimed it.

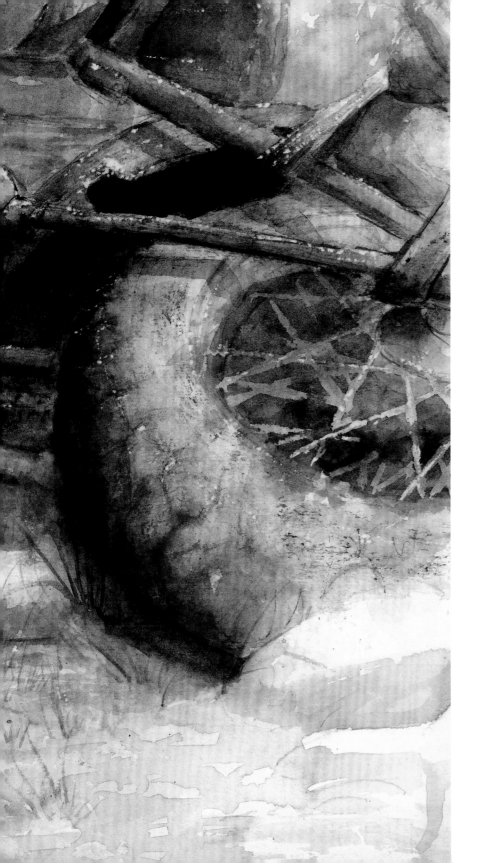

It was sharp and jagged, so I scraped the edges on a flat rock until it was smooth and round like a coin.

T hat little mirror soon became my favorite toy. As I went about my growing up, I carried it with me wherever I went. I was fascinated by the fact that I could so easily reflect and direct the brilliant light of the sun.

I n the beginning it was just a toy. I made up fun games with friends and created challenges for myself.

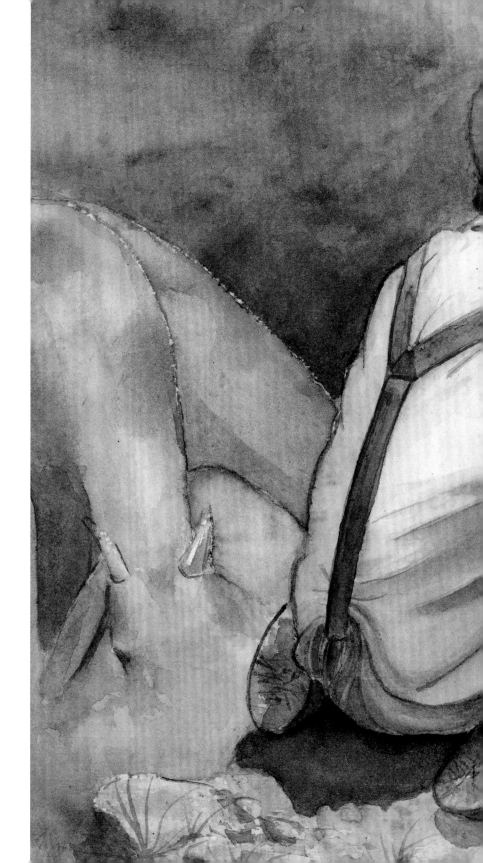

*T*he greatest challenge was to reflect light into dark places where the sun would not shine – in deep holes, rocky crevices…

r the dark corners of closets.

I loved the challenge of getting light into the most inaccessible places I could find, banishing darkness with my reflected light.

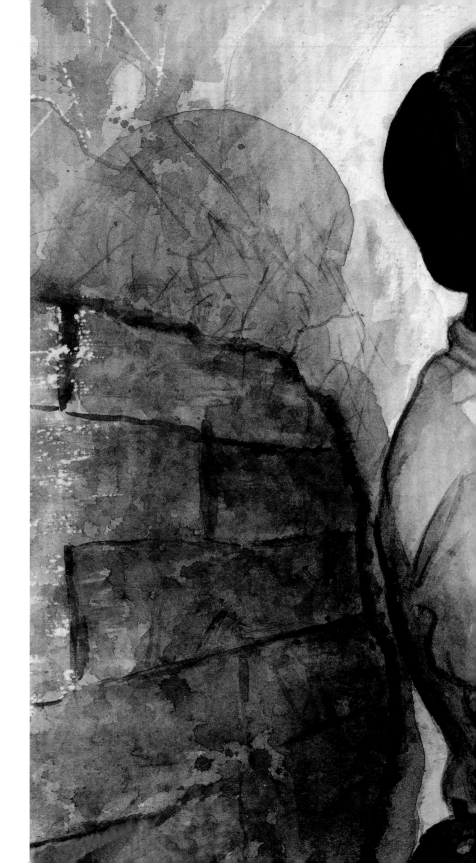

G radually, I came to realize that this was not just a child's game; it was a metaphor for what I might do with my life, and the type of person I could be.

I also came to understand that I am not the light or the source of light.

That light is there, and will only shine in many dark places when I choose to reflect it.

We are fragments of a mirror whose whole design and shape we do not know. Nevertheless, with what we have, we can reflect light into the dark places of this world – into the minds and hearts of others. Perhaps when they see this light, they will do likewise.

After Grandpa finished, the kids were silent for a moment, trying their best to understand. Then Jacob spoke, "I am not sure I understand, Grandpa... How does that help us decide what we want to do when we grow up?"

Grandpa replied, "The story of Alexander Papaderos invites us to change the question from asking what we might want to do when we grow up to what type of person we want to be as we grow up."

"I loved the challenge of getting light into the most inaccessible places
I could find, banishing darkness with reflected light."
Alexander Pasadena

ISBN 978-1-7923-2874-9

No matter what work you decide to do, you can always be someone who reflects light into the lives of others as you do it; and, like young Alexander Papaderos, you can start practicing today."

And, with that, Grandpa handed each child a small, round mirror.

Reviewing storyline and layout with artist Bill Sturgess

THE STORY BEHIND THE STORY

"If you wish to change your story, change your stories." My friend, Brad Barton often shares this insightful bit of wisdom as he encourages people who want to change their circumstances, to change the stories they tell themselves and to each other. The power that stories have to shape our thinking, our workplaces and our day to day lives is as strong today as it was 10,000 years ago – or whenever the first story was told.

An important part of my work helping leaders improve their workplace culture is to invite them to be more intentional and constructive with the stories they share, and the frequency with which they share them. We more easily inspire and invite change in others with stories that inspired change in us. The best stories are the ones that impact us personally– the ones that change the way we see problems, people, and situations. Such stories help bring us clarity on how we may enhance our lives and those of others. They elevate our thinking, increase our confidence, inspire us to believe and behave at a higher level.

The stories that have changed me are the ones I have most compelled to share– and publish. Alexander's Mir is just such a story.

After the surprising success of my first two books, The [Poop Initiative and The Cookie Thief, friends asked w the next story might be. This was not a tough question knew immediately it was the story of Alexander Papade and his mirror. This story moves and changes me every ti I read it – or even think about it! I discovered this delig ful story while reading Robert Fulgham's book, It was Fire When I lay down on it. Robert's stories are typica short, wonderfully told, and usually inspired by real eve I wondered if the story he told about Papaderos was a t story and, if so, I wanted Robert's blessing to re-tell it an illustrated book. I called him, and wrote to him, never heard back. Though frustrating, this turned out be a blessing. After multiple attempts to contact Fulgha I concluded it just wasn't meant to be. Sharing my frus tion with a friend, I told him I had abandoned the proje He looked at me quizzically and asked me a simple,

Knee to Knee with Papaderos at Institute he founded in Gonia

Celebrating Greek Orthodox Easter at Papaderos childhood home with his family

century ago. We visited his childhood home where he lived at the time of the German invasion. He took me to the place where he had discovered the wrecked motorcycle and its broken mirror, and even to the hillside cavern where he first reflected light into darkness. At the days end, Mr. Papaderos invited me to come to his home and enjoy the Greek Orthodox Easter holiday with his family. It was a sacred and special day. He told me that I was the first westerner that he had ever taken to any of these places. We talked about how I came to know of him, and how his story had impacted and inspired me. I showed him the sketches and ideas for the book you are now holding and asked him if I could share this story so it could inspire others as it had inspired me.

He listened carefully to my request, clarified and corrected some details of the story as I had understood it from Fulghum's writings then, to my great astonishment, drew from his old leather wallet a small rounded mirror, the very one from his childhood. Chuckling at my delight he reflected a spot of bright, warm light onto my cheek, and into my heart, saying, "Yes, of course, you may share my story."

found, question: "Why don't you just ask Mr. Papaderos self?" My dismissive reply? "Because it's an old story ut an old guy whom I'm sure is dead by now." My nd rolled his eyes at my weak response. He turned on heel and walked away, returning shortly with an email dress of the administrative assistant who worked at the titute on the Island of Crete where Mr. Papaderos still s, still) lived and worked.

Papaderos "didn't do email" and communicating ough his office wasn't getting me anywhere. With the couragement of friends, however, my frustration transmed into determination, and through a series of serentous events, I was able to fly to the Island of Crete, sit ee to knee with Mr. Papaderos in the institute where he ight.

er he told me the details of the story as it actually happned, he took me on a guided tour of the island of Crete. e reverently stood at mass gravesites and memorials of er wartime atrocities that had taken place over a half

He pulls out the very mirror of his childhood!